W9-ACT-045

Day and Night

by Robin Nelson

Lerner Publications Company · Minneapolis

Day follows night. Night comes after day.

What makes this **cycle** of days and nights happen?

Earth spins in space.

In the morning, your part of Earth is turning to face the sun.

You see the first light from the sun at **dawn**.

The sun rises into the sky at **sunrise**.

It is day.

You can see the sun and
clouds in the sky.

Earth keeps spinning.

In the evening, your part of Earth is turning away from the sun.

The sun moves lower in the sky at **sunset**.

You can no longer see the
sun at **dusk**.

It is night.

You can see the moon and stars in the sky.

Earth turns. The sun will come up again in the morning.

The cycle goes on and on.

Day and Night

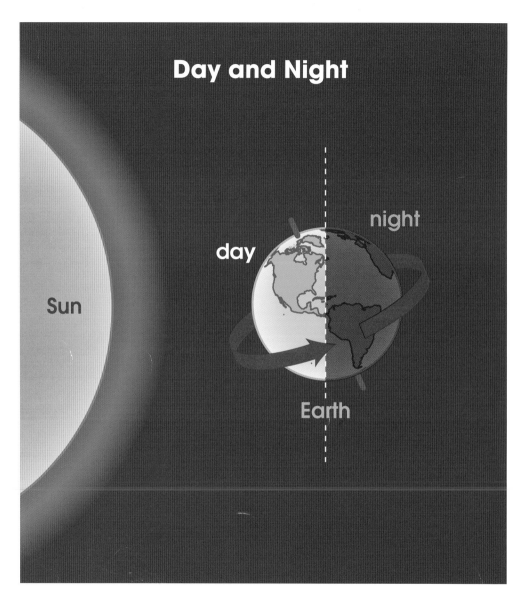

Learn More about Day and Night

Earth spins. It takes Earth 24 hours to spin around once. During about half of those hours, your side of Earth is facing the sun, and it is day. During the other half, your side of Earth is facing away from the sun, and it is night.

Day and Night Facts

 It takes 24 hours for Earth to spin around one time. This is one day.

 The sun always rises in the east.

 In the morning, as Earth spins, the sun rises higher in the sky.

 At midday, the sun is highest in the sky.

In the afternoon, as Earth spins, the sun sinks lower in the sky.

 The sun always goes down in the west.

 When it is day, it is night on the other side of Earth.

Glossary

 cycle – something that happens over and over again over time

 dawn – the time of day when the sun first can be seen

 dusk – the time of day after the sun can no longer be seen

 sunrise – when the sun rises in the sky

 sunset – when the sun moves lower in the sky

Index

The images in this book are used with the permission of: © Galyna Andrushko/Dreamstime.com, p. 2; © Zheng Dong/Dreamstime.com, pp. 3, 22 (top); NASA/JSC, p. 4; © Kinn Deacon/Alamy, p. 5; © Ashley Whitworth/Dreamstime.com, pp. 6, 22 (second from top); © Abjeff/Dreamstime .com, pp. 7, 22 (second from bottom); © age fotostock/SuperStock, p. 8; © Carlos Caetano/ Dreamstime.com, p. 9; © Antonio M. Rosario/Iconica/Getty Images, p. 10; © Stephen Finn/ Dreamstime.com, p. 11; © Titania1980/Dreamstime.com, p. 12; © Darrin Klimek/Taxi/Getty Images, pp. 13, 14, 22 (middle); © J. Silver/SuperStock, p. 15; © Julia Shepeleva/Dreamstime .com, p. 16; © Suzanne Tucker/Dreamstime.com, p. 17; © Laura Westlund/Independent Picture Service, p. 18; © Uguntina/Shutterstock Images, p. 22 (bottom).

Front cover: © Dmitriy Gool/Dreamstime.com

Lerner Publications Company
A division of Lerner Publishing Group, Inc.
241 First Avenue North
Minneapolis, MN 55401 U.S.A.

Website address: www.lernerbooks.com

Library of Congress Cataloging-in-Publication Data

Nelson, Robin, 1971–
    Day and night / by Robin Nelson.
        p.   cm. — (First step nonfiction. Discovering nature's cycles)
    Includes index.
    ISBN 978–0–7613–4576–3 (lib. bdg. : alk. paper)
    1. Earth—Rotation—Juvenile literature. 2. Day—Juvenile literature. I. Title.
QB633.N45 2011
525'.35—dc22   2009020613

Manufactured in the United States of America
1 – DP – 7/15/10